Field Guide to Falling

em jollie

Published by Human Error Publishing
Paul Richmond
www.humanerrorpublishing.com
paul@humanerrorpublishing.com

Copyright © 2017
by
Human Error Publishing & em jollie
All Rights Reserved

ISBN:
978-0-9973472-0-3

Front Cover:
Photo: em jollie
Human Error Publishing

Back Cover
Photo: Richard H. Cowles Jr.

Human Error Publishing asks that no part of this publication be reproduced or transmitted in any form or by any means electronic or mechanical, including photocopy, recording or information storage or retrieval system without permission in writing from em jollie and Human Error Publishing . The reason for this is to help support the artist.

"There's no prayer like desire."
~ Tom Waits

For all the Junipers in the world, and for the Juniper within each of us. For the Medicine carried within longing.

Table of Contents

Field Guide to Falling ... 8

1: step quickly ... 9

How to Crack a Watermelon Open ... 10
Longing, a Sea Dock ... 11
Staying Put ... 12
Grit ... 13
Narrative Fallacy ... 14
As a Consequence of Dreaming ... 16
Sitting Up, Solstice ... 17

2: it's cold, keep moving ... 19

How to Set a Firefly Free ... 20
Notes on Letting Go ... 21
Object Constancy ... 22
After One Month ... 23
Sweet Unravelings ... 24
How to Keep Hungering ... 25
Notes to an Inconvenient, Disobedient Heart ... 26

3: forget the lock ... 29

Ferocious Fruit, or How to Eat Cherries ... 30
Blue Hour ... 31
Blue ... 33
Filling Furrows ... 35
Impermanence/Infinity ... 36
Subtext ... 37
Unspoken ... 38

4: unlearn what you know   41

Impressions Overlooking Paradise Pond   42
Soft Animal   43
On the Many Meanings of Reading   44
Beveled Rainbow   45
A Few Desires, or How to Hunger   46
Fulcrum Point, or How to Cap a Well   47
Belonging, or How to Believe in the Light   49

5: shuttered heart free   51

Dyad   52
How Not to Break   53
Baskets, Woven   54
How to Gaze   56
Greenhouse Carrots   57
Slivers of Yes   58
Wings, or How to Arrive...   59

**Field Guide to Falling:
How to Begin When Beginning is Impossible**

1. Step quickly on icy surface.
2. After all, it's cold. Keep moving to stay warm.
3. Forget to lock your rib cage.
4. Unlearn what you know of vulnerability, go ahead,
5. slip: bloom your shuttered heart free.

1: step quickly

How to Crack a Watermelon Open
or
Portrait of Woman as Girl Inconveniently in Love
(after Robert Walicki, after Neruda)

Allow your eyes to rest on ground. Remind them
not to get stuck on *that one spot*. Scan until you find

a rock, edgy and sharp. It won't be hard, this place
is littered with them. Put campfire out. At least, pretend

it is possible to put fire out. Lean right, as far as you can
away from the beating, beating, beat in left side chest.

Hold both ends firmly. Grasp with all fingers. Encourage
falling faster than

gravity. When surface of green moon splits, notice
how rind pales. How its light turns red. Do not

make friends with her boyfriend. You could, of course,
it may appear easy from outside. You'll quickly discover,

however, stitches in your heart, Inuit bone needle searing
dark soot lines through flesh. Let it tattoo you.

It's a story you can wear forever, like one of those
sacred grandmothers. Make of the pain a palace

of poetry. Never mind the juices dripping
through your fingers. They are deliciously chilled.

Though it is blazing summer, feel their ice. Let
the pink sweetness dissolve

on your tongue.

Without considering what they could grow: Spit out seeds.

Longing, a Sea Dock

Raft has left shore. Almost visible on horizon,
is it coming or going?

Nothing says you must read
what is in front of you now, though I hope
you will. Still, these words cannot tell
you how many times I speak your name
aloud just to hear syllables roll
around in silence, a scatter
of tongue-dropped marbles
on sun-dry wood.

Once, a spiritual teacher said
to me -- *Follow the longing,
it is a guide.* I've tried.
It brings me back to you
every time.

Root of these words burns through veins, firing
everything I cannot say into language anyway,
dam
sprouts
minuscule
leak
before
all the flood rush rush rushes out.

Raft has left shore. I know it will not carry me
home, whether it is coming or going.
I must look for it anyway --
Sometimes the only tether
is to float in longing
brighter than water.

Staying Put

We say: *giving notice*. We think: *two weeks, thirty days*,
always some kind of *leaving*. Walking away

from your door requires more faith than Fall --
Yes, the leaves will brown into dirt before
trees sprout new growth in Spring's arms,
but will I see you again? And soon?

Not calling you my own is the deepest shattering
I have known, and yet like a shard of glass
I can hold it up to the sky. As long as I do so gingerly,
it does not cut my fingertips.
It magnifies the light.

How come holding on requires so much
letting go? When Tara Brach says *The love
is never lost -- It just returns in another form.*
I don't think this is what she means. *You,*

always *you.* I keep wanting. And even if I cannot
have you, you keep appearing. Abundance

begins with empty palms, open arms.
Someone comes, hands me a cup full
like a gift with my portion of morning and I am
drinking sun. For a moment, we are together.

I say *notice* and I mean *doorframe, present, presence* --
the desire to stay forever with that thaw in your eyes.

Grit

How do I get to know the desire
clinging to your
deepest capillaries?
I want to lick your taproot clean.

My neighbor says the leaf mulch
rotting beneath snow
is *disgusting*. It is *rich*, I add.

What I don't say: I imagine
taking it between my palms,
rolling its glorious grit across
my skin,
spreading it with bare fingers,

making seeds blossom.

Narrative Fallacy

Story: everything has some truth in it.
Poetry: put the work out, let it speak.
Science: pheromones, genetics, biology.
Only the facts: you, me, love.

You, me, love: even these raise questions.

Bluebird brings truth, if Spring counts as such.
Though it wasn't Spring, it was Summer
that first time I saw you
through third floor library window
and lost you --

on your way to the parking garage? I rushed downstairs
too slowly. Yet in breathing the air
where you had so recently walked,
I named you. Named you
as if there was no power in it.
As if calling you something

didn't also call you to me. It took chapters
stacked into many years, but we finally met
in the grammar of dailiness. Sentence structure,
meant to keep us from chaos,
also circumscribes the dance.

They say that in love, but not in science,
narrative fallacy -- the tendency
to construct a story around facts --
can serve a purpose. As long as
we don't try to go back
and fabricate facts based on our narrative,
we won't confuse ourselves. Though maybe

what we humans need is more
willingness to be confused,
to blend *what is* with *what can be*.
It was all these seasons

and bluebirds later that we finally met.
That morning, full of glass and light like an apiary,
full of wings and flight. We fly. We fall.
We fly. We fall. *Magic* meets
responsibilities, expectations.
But those, too, are only stories. Where we go from here
depends on what story we are willing to tell
ourselves. If we tell it one way, we get one thing.
Tell it another way, it becomes

something else. Always becoming.
This, our poetry.
Only the facts: you, me, love.
These, our questions.

As a Consequence of Dreaming

I open my eyes, your smell on my skin, lavender
with a touch of something deeper -- pine? And in my limbs
a shimmer of possibility that lingers until I pass the threshold
into full awake morning sun smell of coffee.
As a consequence of dreaming I believe in a road
that leads to flight, your fingers as feathered as wingtips
You have reached your hands into my belly, I have let
my life pour into them, every ventricle, every vein.
As a consequence of dreaming I know I want
to do the same for you, so I hold on
even while letting go. As a consequence of dreaming

I wake up hoping for maple syrup
yet find my hands full of Bittersweet leaves
that will fall
one by one, as seed pods ripen red, orange,
on these vines I will weave
into fire-bright wreath of solitude.

Sitting Up, Solstice

One night I climbed a spiral stair case up,
up into rooms made of starlight where dreams
that can't exist together are all in once place.

The only way to enter the song is *gently*, like chickadee
appears on ash branch. Even the drum has to have some flight

about it. Especially the drum. Spiral staircase up, up,
up out of my body into the nightscape. Where is that

thing I chased, trying to be free? The one that caused
such anguish? It has let me go, set my boat adrift

into a speckled sky of bliss. Nothing left to want.
All night the *maybe* of us turns over in my palm, a piece

of rose quartz catching flame orange motion in its stillness.
Drum beat connects with the heart of this stone, pulses

my hand open, closed, open. *Maybe* is its own prayer.
All night my hips scream to my other joints in a language

I don't understand, though I am trying to listen.
Your touch echoes through the shouts --

This unfettered desire, this paean to freedom.

2: it's cold, keep moving

How to Set a Firefly Free

Just as I am about to fall asleep, something wakes me.
A light. Isn't that the way. *Shine shine flash. Flash.
Shine.* Firefly, suddenly setting aflame cut crystal hanging
from ceiling fan pull-chain. Greenish glow in each facet
while all night white dogwood salts dark-wet sidewalk,
flowers ripped gloriously open in rainpour.
If only I could throw down tears like petals, wear tatters so regally. If
only I could cry blossoms for joy's sake and feed them to us forever,
tangle us in hammock of nourishment. We once reached for one
another, even if it got lost in
translation between your chest and mine. Remember? When old
Tom walked his snarling dog, jerked at chain leashed to spiked
collar, we said they were so mean they belonged together. Yet there
was something sweet about the belonging. When such sweetness
as ours does not belong together, there is some mean stripe about
it. The world bares its teeth.
I watch us recede, become strangers. I want
to bare my teeth back. But there is nothing left
to ask for except acceptance of what is. Slowly,
with an amazing amount of resistance,
I raise myself from bed. Watch my fingers stretch towards
those vibrating wings. Watch
my heart want for a moment to keep it
in my room, even knowing it would fade
and go out by morning. If only it wouldn't. Watch arms reach
for window's top frame. Pull down
sash. See it fly. If only
I didn't know why lightning bugs blink.
If only I wasn't so wise to the fact that your light
does not belong to me, will not ever.
If only I didn't know that was right.

Notes on Letting Go

Skin just beginning to show age wrinkles softening
edge of your clavicle. While explaining the location
of an acupuncture point, the word *clavicle*
rolling casually off your tongue. The places your tongue
has touched on my body. *Irreparable*, so much
like *irreplaceable*, comes to such a different conclusion.
These seven years dreaming distilled, trestle bridge over
muddied ice rendered into a month of trembling endings.
Collective wreckage in cold water. What is that koan
about endings also being beginnings? I can't remember
how it goes as I load the meditation bench into my trunk,
leave
the futon and washer/dryer we finagled through
the tiny cabin door. You wanted so much to keep them.
If you couldn't keep me. Let us find the edges
of every other life we could have lived but didn't. Never mind
the one story, let others creep in to the telling. Let it blur,
while we cast about in darkness, this whole
harmonious song, all the right chords,
played just a single fucking fret off.

Object Constancy

Sand can be grasped in a palm, yes. But wind
will take it eventually. Heart is body's hourglass,
holding its own beginning
& end, its constant ticking tipping moment into
granular moment, for a while. You could take my skull
in your hands, but you will have to give it back
at some point. As will I.

Sure, Freud's nephew came to understand
that Teddy Bear was just over edge of crib when it
disappeared from sight. But where is that Teddy now,
if not in some museum, curators desperately
fighting its inherent impermanence? Presence has to be
interrogative, doesn't it, rather than declarative?
Dust is still dust. What I mean is: how
do I trust more than what I learned in the chaos
of childhood when since then I've been ingrained with loss
upon loss, like every human walking wings of light
through time?

Feather the paintbrush of my fingers across your jaw.
Feather the paintbrush of your fingers across my jaw.
We color each other for this moment. Just this one.
Then it's done, days like hungry teeth devouring
endless could-have-beens into the finite sacred what-was.
I say: I love you (I have no choice)
What I mean to say: I let go (I have no choice)

After One Month

we have run out of tears so we weep
blood that feeds many moons
in shining soil, tidal hearts planted
deep. Color me

marooned in an ocean
of blue   Reaching for the raft
of your cheekbones,
glowing seed of smile.

Maybe this canyon between us isn't something
either of us truly wants. Maybe it came unannounced,
unchosen, because you cannot say more

than what you have already spoken.
The way I can never truly tell you the thrum
of heart's shivering, how after you'd gone
I let my fingers slide over the wooden arm of that old chair,
how I sat just to feel you there.

Maybe I arrived to you unannounced, unchosen
because the universe could not say she loved you
in any other way you would have heard.

Now crescent in the sky has grown full,
then waned

one full cycle since I had any good excuse
to step into your orbit.

Sweet Unravelings, in Your Absence

I walk the streets, unquenchable
footsteps, even with their winter riffs --
coldest chords against my ears. I walk

in early morning, corneas collect glitter
of sun on salt, save it for later. Mid-afternoon,
gray taste of clouds against tongue, ravens

in my hair. After dark the wind hunches each
shoulder, until I look like I am leaning on myself,
rib cage not enough protection. Still, I walk

in your absence: the torture of beauty, sunset
that knifes through eyes, all the way deep
into chest. Sweet slices: I can find nothing

that is not you. Song, shine, silence,
heartbeat. All you. How the infinity of motion
has me convinced, just for a moment,

there is no such thing as loss.

Detritus, or How to Keep Hungering

Arm to arm, sitting at edge of stream
At edge of dream
I leave behind the things I must do

without. I want to better understand
this body you store all your light in.
How we sit, side by side,
with a nourishing picnic between our spines.

If I eat them by the handful I don't see
the miracle of each blueberry -- the whitish flush
on this one, how red blush catches the light
in an extra dimple on that one.
Cherry, clementine, pomegranate. Same story.
Move slowly, slowly. Notice it all.
The crush of juices staining dirt. The bright
orange flesh with its tiny brown bruise of stars.

The graying hairs, a slight sadness at the corner
of your smile. Each tiny asymmetrical miracle.
Finally, how we shake our limbs loose. How
we head to our separate houses.

How the cast off bits of peel & seed,
the only monument we have left,
will soon be washed into water.

Notes to an Inconvenient Disobedient Heart

1.
In the lake of time between
dreaming and waking, when I say it is you
I always look for, and find, it must be you
I mean, though the reflection sometimes looks
like her: No ripples, clear to depth.

2.
Above the lake the horizon appears kindled, like it should be
crackling with flame. What this gracious tugging feeling wants
is a betrayal of so many things. Yet to ignore the craving
is a betrayal of something larger, even more sacred,
and without a name.

3.
Sometimes the ego, the small
conditioned self wants to hate that feeling, the ability
to want. But it is too beautiful, so much shine the urge
to hate can't help falling away, leaving
just this gently terrible longing.

4.
Whatever happens, we can keep the feeling.
Let that desire pull me onward,
to either shore. Dreaming, waking,
dreaming awake again. If it is all mind, the stillness matters.
From it, birth. Like the lifelight that peeks forward
each solstice.

5.
Shh, I keep telling you, inconvenient disobedient heart,
quiet down. You just smile irreverently, say *There never was,
never has been, won't ever be an explanation
for dawn.* Maybe, someday, a spring time, when I will grow
into understanding.

3: forget the lock

Ferocious Fruit,
or
How to Eat Cherries with Someone Who Cannot Be Your Lover

1. Tread lightly. This is dangerous territory.

2. Even if you want to, do not ask if she can tie stems in knots using only her tongue.

3. Do not disclose your status around said skill, whatever it may be.

4. Do not think metaphorically. To be safe, stay away from all similes involving fruit.

5. Do not quote Pablo Neruda. Neither original nor translation.

6. I repeat, do NOT quote Neruda --

7. Especially: *"Quiero hacer contigo lo que la primavera hace con los cerezos"*

8. Tell her about ceremony, how black cherries are for breaking fasts.

9. Do not ask her if she wants to break-fast with you.

10. Make sure the pits you spit out don't touch, or use separate bowls to collect them.

11. If they do touch, don't think about the mingle of saliva.

12. Discuss the sweetness, but only in a general way.

13. Do not read her this poem.

Blue Hour
Sometimes, we cannot bear the thing we crave. ~
Melissa Febos

Six years ago, on my way to the gas station, the grocery store, the coffee shop, the post office, the bank, to see a friend (though not in that order,) I drove by your house five times, at least two and probably three of which were unnecessary.

I was almost on empty, I'd run out of eggs, I needed a hot tea to warm my hands, a letter to Abby who I've known since college needed a stamp, I had a check to deposit. Maybe so many shortcuts were necessary.

But maybe also it was that you were standing in the kitchen of your large Victorian, doing dishes, framed by the windowsill and the failing light – what photographers call "the blue hour," when everything is perfect, and dying.

Your face glowed golden behind the glass. I won't say how indescribably beautiful you were.
I don't want to be improper.

I could see your arms moving, which is how I guessed you were doing dishes. Otherwise I wouldn't have known the sink was there – it was below the level of the window, and I've never been in your house.

I imagined your long fingers holding – what kind of plates? Simple? Round? White? Porcelain? I imagined you picking up the sponge – was it the yellow kind with green bristles on the back?
The soap, smelling of – what, lavender? Citrus?

And of course from there I imagined the ring on your left hand – silver, it bears an emerald. It does not bother me, no more than the ring on my hand. I am not bothered by the fact that, like me, you are a mother with a family to tend.

What I am stuck on is the dishes – such a small, intimate detail.
But it digs into me, this not knowing what they look like.
And, not knowing, I go on my way.

Blue

"The world is blue at its edges and in its depths. This blue is the light that got lost. Light at the blue end of the spectrum does not travel the whole distance from the sun to us. It disperses among the molecules of air, it scatters in water... the light that gets lost gives us the beauty of the world, so much of which is in the color blue..."
~ Rebecca Solnit

Slimmest smile in cerulean sky, tiny moon rises. Falls.
The entire way in blue. Day break, blue shift, what I yearn for
but cannot have. The hue of you. All the while I notice:
weight gravity makes of a child in my arms, pucker taste
of berries on tongue, salt breeze licking my face with sea.
Truro in summer. These overflowing blessings. All day
sun settles on skin, grows a garden of browns.
Then in tan sand the flame angel of sunset. And how
I sit under stars with that small oval of frosty glass
you gave me clasped in my palm. Tears on face catch light
from other side of bay then crawl down my cheeks
like fireflies. Each sob begins selfish, roiling water
in which I miss
you, want you to be mine (whatever that means), want you
to want me to be yours (whatever that means).
But each sob breaks
more easily, ends
with a wash of pure gratitude
for how you unlock the cage
around my chest. Open it wide.
I smell pine sweetness of juniper
tree branches in wind. If you were here,
I'd harvest their berries.
Make tea. Hand you a warm cup. Lean in.
But for now, beyond
parabolic dunes ocean song in dark navy rocks me
to this solitary cry. All this longing,
as if we don't already belong
to one another -- as we are. As if the world is not enough.
As if the light that got lost isn't also a gift.

From this gorgeous place of wave, crash, expanse,
I make the only promise I am allowed to make you, the promise
I'm bound to keep whether I want to or not: this desire may wax full
and yet be hidden as our luna behind other side
of teeming earth, but will never fade. Will orbit
that veined and beating planet between my ribs always.
Even when pale periwinkle, you remain.
You are forever the blue blue palimpsest that shines through. That
gives my world its whole beauty.

Filling Furrows

Fog fills all the furrows -- field, forest, road,
until in the softness I am reminded of the year
I lived in an aquarium of tears, undone,
trapped in wild brine. Met you. Kindly yet surely
you told me to pull myself out, dry up.
By which you meant "remember to laugh."
And I would have, except I wanted you
so keenly my lips wept light. I tilted my head,
opened my mouth for song, but it filled
like a birdbath reflecting sky. What is this blue
I said to myself. Only to myself -- an interrogative
with no question mark, no request for a listener.
Stripe of loss suddenly gave way
to teeth-chattering desire, circle of vibrance.
If I could not have you, then, I decided I would
just keep driving. Until stars appear
like shining music notes, until giggles sprout
our bellies like heart beats, until furrowed
absences are filled with resolute joy, until water
washes over and the salt heals true.
Is the Universe supposed to make sense
to the logical mind? Is there anything outside
mystery? Always, whether it is memory
or body -- and what is the difference -- it is you
that pulls me home.

Impermanence, Infinity

"Beloveds don't find one another.
They are in each other all along."
~ Rumi

Electrons travel roughly the speed of light --
Yours, mine, the kitten's, the Tiger Lily's.
Still, somehow, we all fall down. I'm not trying to be

cute. I really want to know the difference
between observing and consuming,
between gravity and love. What it has to do
with the stars. Suppose an inelegant tide
brought us here, the pull of a dark
moon sky. Might we still leave dancing?

I stroke each orange petal stippled with brown,
leave the stamens and their loads of pollen alone.
Then submerge myself in trees, walk
where deep forest plants grow.

I came here to be alone

But even here I cannot set you down,
cannot get over the way your electrons
move at the same vibration as mine.
Yet still we cannot touch.
Yet still we are made of different stuff.

I want to look at you
without quivering.
I want to warm you
until one of us falls down.

I want us to fall down together, to set the sun in us free
without worrying how the light will burn us up.

Subtext, or Unknowns

Never have I seen a mountain
look so gorgeous as that one, whose name I do not know,
along route 91 where, driving south this morning,
I saw her top softly clipped by what was either high fog
or low clouds. Sun bled from rift in white banks,
almost as bright as your eyes. Somewhere in my belly,
the part of me that is earthen, earthbound, I am
intimately familiar with the shape of her summit,
the arc of her peak. Because I have been there,
or because I will go there. Maybe both.
I think about where we are, the trail of words
behind us, the relief map they cover up
and where it leads. Our minds run their fingers
over the peaks and valleys,
hike that landscape together. Soon
we will head home.

Unspoken

"What you seek is seeking you."
~ Rumi

Always I remain aware it could be you --
swell of light pushing itself over mountain's ridge
each dawn, mouth of yesterday's downpour
swallowing maple limbs, that one pentatonic riff
that -- following the robin's trill -- I can't get out of my mind.

How much can we know of what is unspoken? So far
we have not danced together. But I look for you
everywhere. That woman coming through the front doors
of the coffee shop? Too tall. I can tell peripherally, without even
turning my head. Like I learned when I was young,
picking piano notes out of a multi-instrumental, this is an earned
recognition. What did you do to get so deeply into my bones with
barely a touch between us? In this constellation of wanting, the
more I look for you the more you aren't there. Uncovering connection requires zen, the art of allowing for a softness

to what is unsaid, and our ways
of knowing. What I want is your arms around me
though the stars haven't aligned well enough to open
my mouth and tumble out the request.

I like to think you feel it anyway. This desire
that has me curled on the floor, clasping my wide open
heart into my belly aching, so full of beauty
it is on razor edge of pain. I might spend
all of my days from now on wishing
for us to hold one another, as if we don't already.

Says the robin, the mountain, the rain, the light:
You are looking for me too. Like the clovers. Even
in the places where you are not,
I can find you.

4: unlearn what you know

Impressions Overlooking Paradise Pond

This thirst
in the back of my throat
on its way to my heart, unmeasured
thoughts colliding with memory
of college years and first glimpses,
bird songs my grandfather could name
until his ears began their slow
relinquishing of the world,
an ease of wind, and that shine shocking
off water's surface. The path
I used to walk, dangerously, all on my own
at the end of the day. Another different thirst
I ignored, my willingness to overlook you
as I overlooked my truest self,
how far I was from this day, this same stone bench
in this same place, that just sat all those years
while I learned not to relinquish
what of the world belongs to me.

Soft Animal

Touching. Puddle of light. Everywhere
our bodies intersect. Everywhere they do
not. "Yes,"

says the soft animal of my body. "Yes."

Your footprints make their walkabout in my heart,
pumping ventricle to ventricle. I don't mean there is a desert
in my chest, just that you've brought some moisture
to the arid sky I breathe. I didn't want to tell you
I was lost. As if
you couldn't guess. As if you know nothing
about wandering.

If we are all, in the end, downstream
from one another, where do we go
from here? I want to know: when you say
integrity, do you mean following the rules
someone else has laid out, or do you
mean staying true to your own
kaleidoscopic wholeness, however it

turns? Your wholeness? Our wholeness:
Remembering Earth as the present
she is, and our place within it.
Oh, what I wouldn't give to wake

with these stained fingers tangled
in your sweet hair, its starlight whites,
its garden of browns. Precious body
that mirrors the jewel of this planet.
Pomegranate's geometric gems bled
all over the cutting board, all over
my hands that morning before we sat
together. Close enough
in that puddle of light to feel alive
and a little bit hungry.

On the Many Meanings of Reading

I flash the book cover in your direction
so you can see the title. You laugh,
pull the same one from your bag. And there we are
singed sweetly in my mind: laying together,
parallel study time.
Later strolling that path by the brook.
Sometimes I think how turning through a book
is like a long walk in the forest, though in one case the trees
are in my hands and in the other case I am in the hands
of the trees. Or perhaps it is always the latter.
What birds circled in your brain then,
while scanning those printed pages?
Or, more importantly, was there a tumble of flutters
in your heart at the joke I made,
as if it was a joke, that we should get married because
we crave the same texts? I couldn't read
your response. Did you decipher the truth written
in my grin? All I meant was I already know
I love you indefinitely. Like a grandmother spider
during that walk in the woods this stubborn dream
keeps dropping on a thread into the middle
of our conversation, though I have not named it
(neither have you) as it sways in the gentle breeze
of our shared breaths. It's this:
What I want is to reach right into the center of your bliss,

open it forever.

Beveled Rainbow

Morning light

mirror edge shows beveled rainbow.
I think of your touch,

My body be-comes
something else, a star,

a star-fish, a fishing line reeling
You in: closer, closer

Please

The rose quartz that caught
our solstice fire

catches now the sun,
turns that "maybe"

into a yes we arc together.

A Few Desires, or How to Hunger

I want to be the malleable soap
your hands sculpt as you cleanse yourself,
as ordinary and as daily and as caressed as that.

I want to be the cutting board, that firm surface
you can lay edges against, that allows you
to divide roughage from nourishment.

I want to be the pillow case, containing all
the softness for resting your public face
and the slim canvas you play your private dreams onto.

Let me suds into joining the stream of water
down the drain, become the bamboo board
oiled so many times until finally, split, I am

placed on the compost pile. Let the laundry
tear my threads until, like the pillow case,
I cannot contain, but let every thriving thing seep out.

But in truth I can be none of these things,
just this tiny self loving you, accepting your gifts,
providing what sustenance I can in return.

In other words, use me up, until I am done with myself.

Fulcrum Point,
or How to Cap the Well You Once Fell Into

(I)
First, choose
a wood or two -- cherry for the sweet red smell,
sugar maple for how it reminds you of your grandmother
and that tree out your childhood bedroom window.
Plane the grainy surface smooth. Notice
how this act was once impossible,
how every time you tried before -- the wood balked,
split. Now lean backwards (even if counterintuitive
to the carpenter in you who has gotten so good
at constructing

walls). Really lean. Let the point of contact, that bridge
from one real self to another, be a fulcrum. Notice:
leverage, levity. Build from there. With this fulcrum point
you learn your hands suddenly steady. Nothing quite as
heavy
as it once seemed. Make a circle, as close to perfect
as a human can get, which is not very close,
but make it anyway. Sand
it down. Sand,
and sand.
Then place it across top of well. Do not worry
if it wobbles at first. It will grow into place
on mossy stones, irreversibly become part
of the structure. Trust. Know
that from one fulcrum, others may be created.
The architecture is inside you. Once the well is capped,
it is no longer possible to trip & tumble,
to lose yourself down its dark depth.

(II)
Next, choose some seeds. Roses will do,
particularly if propagated from seaside plants
at edge of dunes.
Sprinkle them on ground in a sunwise way around
the whole. Wait. Eventually: green, pink, a dazzle of bees.

Realize the beauty, a buzzing shock of color.

Yes, see, these vines have been growing ease seasons
enough that their hips are full. Remove achenes from
hypanthium, make tea from fruit and plant the rest --
winter them over, grow more flowers that open
into this sustainability, petals that last
and last.

Belonging, or How to Believe in the Light

Six inches above street lamp arm
the crow   hovers,
seems to
        float
for several seconds, wings impossibly outstretched
                        spiny claws extend
before coming to rest

with firm grip around round metal pole.
Feathers flash purple
pennaceous barbs within deep blackness,
sun stencils bird's silhouette
onto brown oak leaves below, yet what I notice
first is the faith demanded by her
descent out
of flight, her willingness
to stop flapping
               and fall

onto her perch.
I think of my younger self, landing strips
that kept disappearing, steel turned
to mist,
to nothingness,
solidity I never learned to trust.
This is why I tell you my story.
You listen

and I can hover
              over what matters,
              pour myself into your palms,
into outstretched wings
of my own palms.
Believe in the light,
become the crow.

5: shuttered heart free

Dyad

In other words: mystery.
In other words: I am in the house alone,
strike a match, see flame on window pane
and my hand reflected. Then, through glass,
across the way, another fire burning
impossibly bright in a midnight of stars
I reach for, yet can only imagine touching.
But that dazzle
is you, holding a torch in your own space,
heart sending lighthouse signal
calls me to my life.
With your words, your breath,
your willingness to pray beside me.
How you meet me in the middle,
center place of diamond resiliency.
In between the days, storms rage
inside, tussle my house open
and there you are, cupping hands,
helping me make sure
(as if anything is sure)
the flame isn't blown out.
Here, I also offer you my palms,
the soft breeze in my chest,
and whatever sun
I have.

How Not to Break,
or Upon Dropping my Bag of Stones

something has broken open --
this ancient ammonite, solidly spiraled for ages
now pours forth its rainbow song

in which your name is another word for sun.
What our bodies do when we touch: bright splatter
in sky forever, feed the whole planet with light.

This is how everything unfurls. This is how everything
changes. It appears perched on the edge of a cliff,
ready to fall and smash to bits. Maybe it does

fall. Maybe it does smash to bits. But then suddenly it is
made out of birds, and you never knew how much flight
was hiding in your veins all this time.

Some people are easier to love, you said, not
objectively but because the part of God they are
is closer to the part of God we are

-- it is all one jigsaw, though we know
the pieces meant to nuzzle our edges.
The way a craggy fossil stone, when shattered,

will only fit together one way, just one way,
placed tenderly jagged to jagged at precisely right angle.

Baskets, Woven
"If I did not know you, I would not have found you."
~ Pascal

Staccato of budding stars above, I am
at the lake walking alone along an edge of water again.
This is a good sign. Brook stumbles its way
over stones – I hear your name in the frets it mutters.
But all I can talk about is baskets
when I try to say your name. What I mean
has to do with holding, how birch bark can contain liquid,
even let it boil over a fire given the right weft
and weave. Your name is birch bark basket
touching singing kettle of my heart.

Off the path made by humans: tracks of Deer, Bobcat.
Trees groan like wounded Moose. Earlier, sun blazed
bright orange on the winter river, snow shone.
Just last week the ice floes spelled a bridge,

now there is only water. I passed it, thought: the light
is too beautiful to photograph. I realize I cannot write you
in this poem, nor with any words. I can only find you
in the rhythm of reeds, the round, receptive

shape of a basket, a certain depth of intuition.
Immediately I recognized you
from the days ahead. You fit exactly into an open space
my heart was yawning.

That Friday I saw you standing
in the driveway I wouldn't have realized it was you
but for the way you arc your body, rainbow cutting
through the dark. You are made of sunlight
and some rain. Though you haven't told me your tears,
I know them in my marrow, as well as I know
the octave where your voice lives, full of rock, full of water.

Like this lapping shoreline, every time
your eyes fall on me I feed
that feeling to my bones.

Four Minutes, or How to Gaze

I wanted to say *begin again*
as soon as time was up, to sit there longer falling
in & out, hues of brown irises meeting in deep & light,
pupils calibrating prayers -- four soft circles making,
for those moments, one sweet whole: medicine wheel
rainbow with arc seen above,
the rest felt below. A language of sunshine we carry
carefully forward. What I thought would be eternity (and it is
foreverness we tasted there), was such a flash
of a moment. I wanted to say

Start the timer again. But since I didn't,
I want to tell you now about the inner space of it.
The outer space of it. The meeting in the middle
of it. Those shared breaths, another dash
of Springtime in our microcosm, this endless circle
of seasons we forge together.

Four minutes that touched
places I hadn't uncovered in years, quenched
the small hard center of longing I carry
beneath the layers of longing I know how to name.
Four minutes that made me remember those words --

Begin again. Begin again. Begin
again. Begin. Again.

Greenhouse Carrots

"There is something too large for language here. Some current of energy flows between them; it is neither maternal nor erotic but contains elements of both. "
~ Michael Cunningham

Dragon-red carrots with vermillion orange insides shown by their cut-off tops. This is the first image I recall upon waking. Am I saving biennial seeds in my sleep?

Then the memory expands: I am in an old-fashioned greenhouse with blue tinted glass, framed by intricate ironwork, shaped fantastically as could only exist in a place of dreams, not governed by gravity. The rooms are terraced.

Several steps below me sparkles a brilliant turquoise pool. Mossy rocks, spotted koi, earth smells, serene running water sounds. Senses engulfed. I look down through the space -- illuminated with rays of light like the ocean -- from where I stand in front of trays of richdark soil. In each tray, an edible plant grows.

I pull the carrots out one at a time, noticing the resistance of their skin against the dirt, the tension of tiny roots relinquishing their hold. I am saving carrots for the root cellar, ferny emerald tops for - yes - seeds.

On a shelf nearby I see the card I wrote you. Though you are not in the room with me, I think of your smile and have a powerful sense of being invited. It seems that either you have just left the interior of the greenhouse or will soon be returning to it. Maybe both things are true. Your presence is palpable. I consider picking up the card so that I might hand it to you, so that our fingers might brush and in that simple, safe touch I could remember how real you are.

Slivers of Yes

We are nothing more than a sliver of yes
between some stars, a shiver of heartbeats

Sometimes the soft is too much, the sweet rain & bird songs
drifting through the window screen, merged into one stream
as they enter my ears

Becomes a lake both fluid and definite,
except in drought or flood when it no longer knows itself
though we call it by the same name

Everyone calls me by the same name today, as if
they cannot see dunes shifting in my chest,
how much of my skin now belongs to your palm.

Wings,
or How to Arrive at a Sense of Completion in an Incomplete World

You are no longer the kind of young that walks the dark path
alone past the pond by the tea house at night. But still
it is your job to open your shoulders, even in the cold.

And if you placed those stones in a solid path
right to the middle of your heart so she could walk in,
your clever masonry was not for her.

No, it was for you. Go ahead,
move, right into the gleam

of your own center.

em's favorite color is turquoise, at least most of the time. She loves to be outside. Her literary work comes from a place in her that believes strongly in social justice with an intersectional lens, and a better world for all.

when to nourish your longing
and when to "spit out the seeds"?
if you have ever savored the stew of desire,
and especially if you have contemplated
when to keep cooking and when to empty
the pot, em jollie is the poet you want at the table
these are sexy, mouth-watering poems
that might break your heart,
but will also feed you heartily
and leave you happy to be alive
in this world, flawed though you are
flawed though this world may be.
-- Sally Bellerose, novelist

Em Jollie's poems show us color, but more than that, her poems expose the depth of color through our other senses. We taste the moving light, hear the green of watermelon rind, feel the brush of blue sky against our skin. Her poems are an implosion of color.
-- John Sheirer, writer/professor

Poems about the inexorability of falling in love. The highs it brings and also some of the lows. When you're in love the world changes, takes on a different feeling. Poems about vulnerability, about opening yourself to let in the light. They're poems about hope and about the twining together of...people...
-- Elizabeth Rosendorf, Architect

[In these poems] there are places of startling clarity and beauty... mixed with brain-splitting twists and turns. Powerful stuff.
-- Melissa Tantaquidgeon Zobel, author of Wabanaki Blues, Mohegan Medicine Woman

"A Field Guide to Falling" tore my heart apart and built it back up in the most endearing way. I could feel the longing we all feel when we want deeply... In these pieces, Jollie reminds us what it was like to feel first love growing, climbing, and settling inside our human hearts. "A Field Guide to Falling" is what all great poetry is--a lifetime in just a few words.
-- Tiffani Burnett-Velez, Writer, Editor

www.ingramcontent.com/pod-product-compliance
Lightning Source LLC
Chambersburg PA
CBHW051710090426
42736CB00013B/2623